Sports Illustrated KIDS

Sports Illustrated Kids: Legend vs. Legend

STEPHEN CURRY

VS.

KOBE BRYANT

BASKETBALL LEGENDS FACE OFF

by Elliott Smith

CAPSTONE PRESS
a capstone imprint

Published by Capstone Press, an imprint of Capstone
1710 Roe Crest Drive, North Mankato, Minnesota 56003
capstonepub.com

Library of Congress Cataloging-in-Publication Data
is available on the Library of Congress website.
ISBN: 9798875218422 (hardcover)
ISBN: 9798875218378 (paperback)
ISBN: 9798875218385 (ebook PDF)

Summary: Stephen Curry has won four NBA championships and two NBA Most Valuable Player (MVP) awards. Kobe Bryant won five NBA championships and four All-Star Game MVP awards. But which is the all-time best? Readers can compare the players and their feats and decide for themselves!

Editorial Credits
Editor: Patrick Donnelly; Designer: Elyse White; Media Researcher: Jo Miller; Production Specialist: Tori Abraham

Image Credits
Associated Press: Ashley Landis, cover (left), David J. Phillip, 24, Jae C. Hong, 14, Matt Patterson, 15, Paul Sakuma, 9, Santiago Mejia/San Francisco Chronicle, 17, Tony Avelar, 21; Getty Images: Ezra Shaw, 13, 25, 27, 29, Harry How, 11, Jason Miller, 19; Newscom: UPI Photo/Jim Ruymen, 20; Shutterstock: saicle (background), cover and throughout; Sports Illustrated: Bob Rosato, 28, Erick W. Rasco, 23, John W. McDonough, cover (right), 4, 5, 6, 7, 12, 16, 18, 22, 26, Manny Millan, 8, 10

Printed and bound in China. 006276

Contents

** * * All stats are current through the 2023–24 NBA season. * * **

Words in **bold** appear in the glossary.

Basketball Legends Face Off!

Kobe Bryant and Stephen Curry both became superstars in the National Basketball Association (NBA). Bryant was known for his all-around game and **intensity**. Curry is one of the most **accurate** shooters ever. Which is the best? Let's see how they match up!

Kobe Bryant

Stephen Curry

THE MATCHUP	Born	State
Kobe Bean Bryant	August 23, 1978	Pennsylvania
Wardell Stephen Curry II	March 14, 1988	Ohio

Height and Weight

A player's size doesn't always matter in basketball. Experts thought Curry was too short and skinny to play in the NBA. But his speed, vision, and shooting make up for his size. Bryant entered the NBA as a wiry teenager. But he got bigger and stronger. He could score against or defend anyone.

Bryant stood tall among NBA guards.

Curry's quickness and body control allows him to slice through heavy traffic.

THE MATCHUP	Height	Weight
Kobe Bryant	6 feet, 6 inches (198 centimeters)	212 pounds (96 kilograms)
Stephen Curry	6 feet, 2 inches (188 cm)	185 pounds (84 kg)

Games Played

Curry was drafted by the Golden State Warriors in 2009. He is the team's career leader with more than 950 games played. The Charlotte Hornets drafted Bryant in 1996. He was immediately traded to the Los Angeles Lakers. Bryant played more than 1,300 games with the Lakers.

Bryant shakes hands with NBA Commissioner David Stern after being drafted by the Hornets.

Curry holds up his new jersey at his first press conference as a Warrior.

THE MATCHUP	Drafted	Games Played
Kobe Bryant	1996 (Round 1, Pick 13)	1,346
Stephen Curry	2009 (Round 1, Pick 7)	956

Shooting

Curry is an incredible shooter. He has amazing **range**. He led the NBA in three-pointers eight times. His 3,747 three-pointers is an NBA record. Bryant also had great shooting range. But he was more comfortable closer to the hoop. He led the league in **field goals** three times. He made 11,719 career field goals. That's seventh on the all-time list.

Bryant displays his perfect shooting form.

Curry (right) launches a three-pointer over the Lakers' Anthony Davis in 2023.

THE MATCHUP	Field Goals	Three-Pointers
Kobe Bryant	11,719	1,827
Stephen Curry	8,084	3,747

Assists

Great passing can lead to more points. Bryant had 6,306 career **assists**. As a point guard, Curry has many chances to pass. He has 6,119 assists. Curry's best season came in 2013–14. He averaged 8.5 assists per game that season.

Bryant looks for an open teammate in a 2014 game against the Memphis Grizzlies.

Curry's pass splits two Houston Rockets defenders during a 2022 game.

THE MATCHUP	Career Assists	Average Per Game
Kobe Bryant	6,306	4.7
Stephen Curry	6,119	6.4

Defense

Quick hands make Curry a **menace** for opponents. He led the league in steals twice. But he has never made the NBA All-Defensive Team. Bryant was one of the best defenders ever. He was named to the All-Defensive Team 12 times.

Bryant goes for the steal against San Antonio Spurs guard Danny Green in 2014.

Dallas Mavericks star Luka Dončić squares off against Curry in a 2022 game.

THE MATCHUP	Steals	Average Per Game	All-Defensive Team
Kobe Bryant	1,944	1.4	12 (1999–2003, 2005–2011)
Stephen Curry	1,473	1.5	0

Rebounding

Guards don't get many chances for rebounds. Curry usually stays outside the **lane**. He grabs rebounds off long missed shots. He averaged a career-best 6.1 rebounds in 2022–23. Bryant muscled into crowds. He averaged more than 6.0 rebounds per game in three seasons.

Bryant jumps for a rebound in a 2014 game.

Curry goes high to grab the rebound against Grizzlies center Steven Adams during the 2022 playoffs.

THE MATCHUP	Rebounds	Average Per Game
Kobe Bryant	7,047	5.2
Stephen Curry	4,509	4.7

Points Scored

Bryant was one of the league's top scorers. He led the league in points per game twice. His career total of 33,643 points is fourth in league history. Curry is a **prolific** scorer too. He also has two NBA scoring titles. Curry is among the top 30 scorers of all time.

Bryant throws down a dunk in 2013.

Curry fires up a long jumper against the Cleveland Cavaliers in the 2018 NBA Finals.

THE MATCHUP	Points	Average Per Game	NBA Scoring Titles
Kobe Bryant	33,643	25.0	2 (2005–06, 2006–07)
Stephen Curry	23,668	24.8	2 (2015–16, 2020–21)

Great Game

Bryant scored 50 points in a game 25 times. His best game was on January 22, 2006. He scored 81 points. Only one player has ever scored more than that. Curry scored at least 50 points in 13 games. On January 3, 2021, he scored 62 points.

Bryant is interviewed after he scored 81 points against the Toronto Raptors in 2006.

Teammate Damion Lee douses Curry with water to celebrate Curry's career-high 62-point game in 2021.

THE MATCHUP	Most Points in a Game	50+ Points in a Game
Kobe Bryant	81	25
Stephen Curry	62	13

Olympic Glory

Curry made his Olympic **debut** with Team USA at the 2024 Paris Games. He averaged 30 points in the last two games. The U.S. won the gold medal. Bryant played in two Olympics. He helped Team USA win gold in 2008 and 2012.

Bryant in action during the 2008 Beijing Olympics

Curry celebrates after helping Team USA beat France in the 2024 Olympic gold-medal game.

THE MATCHUP	Olympic Appearances	Medals
Kobe Bryant	2008 (Beijing), 2012 (London)	2 gold
Stephen Curry	2024 (Paris)	1 gold

NBA Championships

Bryant led the Lakers to the NBA title five times. They won three straight titles from 2000 to 2002. Bryant was named Finals Most Valuable Player (MVP) twice. Curry helped make the Warriors a **dynasty**. He led them to four NBA titles in eight years.

Bryant celebrates winning the title and being named NBA Finals MVP in 2009.

Curry raises the NBA championship trophy during a victory parade in 2018.

THE MATCHUP	NBA Championships	Finals MVP
Kobe Bryant	2000, 2001, 2002, 2009, 2010	2 (2009, 2010)
Stephen Curry	2015, 2017, 2018, 2022	1 (2022)

Honors and Awards

Curry was named NBA MVP in 2015 and 2016. He also was chosen for the All-Star Game 10 times. He was named to the All-NBA First Team four times. Bryant was the NBA MVP in 2008. He was an 18-time All-Star. He made the All-NBA First Team 11 times.

Bryant was named MVP of the 2007 NBA All-Star Game.

Curry poses with his two NBA MVP trophies in 2016.

THE MATCHUP	NBA MVP	All-Star Games	All-NBA First Team
Kobe Bryant	1 (2008)	18	11
Stephen Curry	2 (2015, 2016)	10	4

Who Is the Best?

Bryant and Curry are both legends. Bryant could drive, dunk, and defend anyone. That made him one of the toughest players in NBA history. Curry's amazing shooting lets him score at will from anywhere. But who is the best? You make the choice!

Bryant dunks the ball at the 2008 Olympic Games.

Curry takes a jump shot against the Lakers in 2024.

Glossary

accurate (AK-yu-rit)—on target

assist (uh-SISST)—a pass in sports that leads to a goal or basket

debut (day-BEW)—first appearance

dynasty (DYE-nuh-stee)—a team that dominates its sport for a period of time

field goal (FEELD GOHL)—in basketball, a shot that goes through the hoop

intensity (in-TEN-suh-tee)—great energy or spirit

lane (LAYN)—the area between the free-throw line and the basket

menace (MEN-iss)—a consistent bother or threat

prolific (pro-LIFF-ik)—very productive

range (RAYNJ)—the distance from the hoop a shooter is comfortable shooting from

Read More

Abdo, Kenny. *Basketball GOATs*. Minneapolis: Abdo Publishing, 2024.

Blue, Tyler. *Kobe Bryant*. New York: Abbeville, 2025.

Smith, Elliott. *Stephen Curry: Basketball's Greatest Shooter*. Minneapolis: Lerner, 2024.

Internet Sites

Biography: Stephen Curry
biography.com/athletes/stephen-curry

NBA: Kobe Bryant
nba.com/stats/player/977/career

The Players' Tribune: Kobe Bryant: Dear Basketball
theplayerstribune.com/articles/dear-basketball

Index

About the Author

Elliott Smith is a freelance writer, editor, and author. He has covered a wide variety of subjects, including sports, entertainment, and travel, for newspapers, magazines, and websites. He has written more than 70 children's books both in fiction and nonfiction. He lives in the Washington, D.C., area with his wife and two children.